HMO SUCCESS

A Beginner's Guide to Starting out on a Multi-Let Property Business

By

Marie Ellis

Published in April 2020

<Blank Page>

"The combination of Marie's enthusiasm and experience makes this book a valuable introduction for those entering the HMO market."

Andy Burton, RLA Director 2007 - 2020.

<Blank Page>

Table of Contents

<Blank Page>

Acknowledgements

I would like to dedicate this book to my amazing, beautiful and totally selfless daughter Lily-Jane. We have been through some tough times together and I love you with all my heart.

I would also like to dedicate this book to 'Nanny Powell' (Lilian) who passed away on 31st March 2020.

A big thank you to **Jasim Khazi** for formatting this book and helping me get it ready for publication. I could not have finished it without you.

And to **Georgina Smallwood** my Business Partner for making sure it all came together and for all your help and advice.

<Blank Page>

About The Author

I have been 'in property' all my life, from a young age (17).

I was unfortunate to lose my mom to cancer in 1985 and I was left in a very volatile household (my mom had remarried), having to 'escape' very quickly I found myself homeless. My brother had died five years prior of leukaemia when he was 15. My dad was significantly 'absent'. I was suddenly all alone.

I was propelled into a world of facing life without anywhere to live, bereaved and scared. I remember going to local Letting Agents asking for lists of affordable places for me to live. In those days it was even legal for a Letting Agent to charge someone for a list of properties.

As I was 17, I seemed to slip through the net for everything; no help, no 'priority' at the council and not old enough to sign a lettings contract.

On top of which I had my brother's little dog and there was no way I was parting with her, she was just too special and practically all I had left in the world. My saviour came via my great Aunty 'Kit' who gave me enough money to buy a mobile home. Home it was and I was eternally grateful. It was extremely cold being made entirely of metal and I had to cope with learning how to light a Parkray solid fuel heating system, something I had never had to do before. But in 'survival mode' you just have to get on with it, there is no real choice. There I was in my little haven, glad of any help that neighbours could give me, including an elderly gentleman called George who taught me how to light that fire.

The decision to not be able to continue at school to do A-levels had been made for me, I had to go and earn a living. A friend of mine told me that the local Council were offering Youth Training Scheme places (YTS) which were like apprenticeships on very low pay. I had to do something, so I joined the Council in 1985 and took on a bar job in the local pub to support my income, which I hated.

I progressed through the Council looking after Council house repairs, driving around in a van doing estate management and then becoming ironically, the Homeless Persons' Officer having completed a qualification in the Chartered Institute of Housing in 1991.

I introduced the Private Sector leasing scheme to the Council whereby we housed homeless families into houses instead of bed and breakfast accommodation, saving the Council literally thousands of pounds.

From there I went on to be a Property Leasing Manager at Bromford Housing Association (now The Bromford Group). My job there was to accommodate families from their waiting list, into properties leased from private landlords. I had to arrange 'hand backs' at the lease end and was given a shoe-string budget to do so. Most of the 'damages' done by tenants had to be put down to 'fair wear and tear' which of course they weren't. I am sure things are different now.

When Bromford's funding was cut, I fell across an advert for Residential Services Manager at the University of Wolverhampton. I applied for it, not thinking for one minute I would be successful. Never say Never. Always have faith in yourself. My salary increased significantly. I was on a roll.

My job was huge, looking after 2,000 bed-spaces over initially 5 campuses, as well as inspecting and accrediting all the Student houses (more about that later). The hours were long but the job itself was very satisfying, however as time went on, I was less on the 'front line' and my job became more about writing reports and risk assessments, it just was not the same.

Following the birth of my beautiful daughter in 2003, I decided I wanted to spend more time being an 'at home parent' and gave up my role at the University. It was a hard decision, the money was good, but the hours were long.

In 2006 I set up a Property Management Company called Housemates which I ran from home until 2015 when I opened a Letting Agency and grew my management portfolio including taking on my own investment properties. My Letting Agency was a great success and had a turnover of over £100k from fees that I received from landlords. This goes to show how lucrative property management can be and once you learn how to do this correctly, you can go onto look after other people's HMOs and earn 10-15% per property. This is something else the HMO Training Academy can help you with if you are interested.

I found that I could work property around my life and be an 'at home' parent when I needed to be.

In 2007, just as property prices crashed, I purchased my own HMO (House in Multiple Occupancy) which was done entirely for the purpose of providing funding for Lily when she went to University which is now only 18 months away. Buying a property for her benefit has done just that and enabled me to buy the 'extras' to help her on her way too. For three years' running now she has been performing with her Drama Company 'The Pauline Quirke Academy' on the Royal Mile in Edinburgh and I feel so lucky I have been able to send her there. She also has regular singing lessons and takes part in Open Mic sessions and lead roles in productions at her college.

I purchased another property which was an existing HMO. When Article 4 (see later) was introduced in 2017, this had the effect of increasing its value by over £40k.

Both student houses have accrued over £80k additional equity over ten years and provided £18k per year in income, that is a total of £260,000 additional income from just TWO three bedroomed terraced properties! You can see then just how these HMOs over time can really make a difference to your income and future 'nest egg'.

During the time I owned and operated Housemates, I also took on a portfolio of Rent-to-Rent (R2R) properties to accommodate the 'overspill' when the Agency had run out of student houses. I held those in my own name. Some were extremely successful and some really were not. It was all part of the learning curve.

In 2018, I sold my Lettings agency to another company in Wolverhampton, for a six-figure sum. I was so proud of what I had achieved but it was time to do something else.

I decided to take some time out, after all I had never had any from the age of 17, so I thought it was a good time to regroup, reflect and retrain.

I have since invested in myself by becoming a compliant Deal Sourcer, I paid a significant amount to learn how to do it properly. I have worked with a national company selling HMOs and sold large properties to both UK and overseas investors.

My passion has always been HMOs and I do sometimes miss that part of my life. So now I have decided to teach other people how to make a genuinely nice income from property, achieving income from those that you own and those that you do not.

Let me show you how.

Chapter 1 – Introduction

Legal Definition of an HMO

This is a Housing Act classification for a house (or flat) with 3 or more occupants, forming 2 or more households

For example, a 2-bed flat with a couple and an unrelated friend in the 'spare' room would be an HMO and subject to HMO regulations

Who is this Book for?

This book is for people who are interested in property and may have some background and an understanding of what HMO investment can really do for you. Done properly, it can bring in an additional stream of income into your household and eventually you may be able to make the leap away from the day job. Alternatively, it may provide an income for a stay at home parent as once you are up and running, much of it can be done part time. I know, I have done it.

Once you have built up your knowledge and expertise and are running properties profitably and compliantly for yourself, there is no reason why you cannot manage for other people and look after their HMOs. There is certainly a shortage of people doing it properly. On average the 'management fee' is around 10-15% which can build up nicely, particularly if your 'patch' is condensed in an area you can get to quickly.

There is a lot to learn and you cannot do it all from reading this book or looking at YouTube videos, there is just too much at stake. You must know all the ins and outs and know when you can get caught out, where you could make mistakes which could close your business down. We will cover some of the compliance issues in this book but that is another book to write.

Why did I write this book?

I have seen it so many times, people getting it wrong and taking on deals that just do not work. I have done many consultations and mentorships when we have looked at the area, the property, the demand, the business case, the figures just do not cut the mustard. I have seen people get nasty fines from the council and have lost everything. Rather than learning the hard way, my aim is to get investors doing this properly and to learn from the mistakes of others (including mine). The chapter on 'My Council Fine' experience makes startling reading.

Taking the decision to buy this book is a fabulous first step as a new HMO investor. I guarantee you will get your investment back many times over.

There are so many money saving tips and tricks in here to enable you to do just that.

If you dream about being 'financially free' after a few months or having 'passive income' then as many investors will tell you, that is not going to happen quickly at all. It takes time, patience, knowledge and planning to get you there. Property management/ownership is certainly not 'passive' as it involves hard work. Even when you have your HMO and hand it on to an agent, you are not 'off the hook', as you always need to know what is going on. **THE LEGAL RESPONSIBILITY FOR YOUR TENANTS IS ALWAYS YOURS WHETHER YOU HAVE AN AGENT OR NOT.** So, it is important you know what is going on all the time and stay ahead of the game.

How this Book will help you

I have packed this book with hints, tips and case studies to help you on your way. Many of them have been learned from my own experience, things that mainstream training will not teach you; the good, the bad and the ugly. This book is not designed for you to read it then go out straight away and become a No. 1 property person. Combine it with training and mentorship. Continuous learning is always key. Things change demographics, laws, rules and regulations and people's expectations. Grow with it and keep yourself up to date. I can only tell you the reality of the 'here and now' but it is a fabulous foundation to get you going.

It will help you:

- Identify profitable property
- Understand the two high return property strategies
- Get your property cash-flowing quickly and easily
- Deal with agents and landlords
- Find ideal tenants
- Find out what pitfalls to avoid
- Learn the basics of what you are going to need to know to be a success

CHAPTER 2 - THE DEMAND FOR HMOS

In the Olden Days

Dingy, poorly lit, poorly maintained and uninviting rooms. Usually with a bare mattress, very often stained. Central ceiling light, bedside table and melamine wardrobe. And brown curtains. And rude and unhelpful 'jobsworth' security staff.

Those images are still etched in my memory and I remember them clearly from my first job at the University (as Residential Services Manager) when all the students used to arrive at their new 'digs' in halls and queue around the block awaiting their keys. They would unlock a dingy bedroom, painted magnolia, with a single bed and little else. Parents would empty their Citroen people carriers and cart in loads of stuff to make their offspring's rooms just a little more homely.

Back then if someone was interested in renting a room in a house or better still a whole group wanted to live together, they would shuffle into the Accommodation Services HQ (a few rooms in the Halls buildings, equally dull) and be given a Word document with lists of landlords in the area who 'qualified' to rent their home to University students.

And I should know, I had to go and inspect them all as part of my job as well as making sure all the Uni rooms were full. Big job. Not bad money but long hours.

A lot has changed since then. When I arrived in 1998, I realised that things had to change. We turned some dingy rooms into 'show rooms', upgraded the advertising, put on Open Days, had Opening Events with lots of interesting things going on and best of all got rid of that awful Word document and joined the 21st century with an Internet based system. Hooray.

Times do change and so do trends, things cannot always stay the same and people, including landlords must change with the times. There have been many challenges, changes in legislation, tax rules (landlords having to pay more of it), more new build Purpose Built Student Accommodation (PBSA), more choice, more competition, new ideas, stuff to get students (and professionals) excited about their new homes, gyms, games rooms, swimming pools, chill out areas, bars... and the list goes on

Where I live and work, in Wolverhampton, more students are choosing to live in the Uni halls or halls provided by the private sector. First years do not always fit into shared housing that well as they can be just too, well, let us just say they need too much support and things can go so wrong. In their second year and beyond, things are a lot better; they have learned a lot about communal living.

Professional Tenants – Our New Buddies

Over the last five to ten years there has been an emergence of a different kind of HMO market, seen as plugging the gap when renting an entire flat or house is unaffordable. Postgrads very often want to stay in the shared house scene as their experience has hopefully been a good one and they are keen to not go home to mom and dad. But renting a complete property may not be an option on a graduate wage.

There has been a demographic shift into shared houses and now the competition is on. More and more 'No Money Down' courses or 'Passive Income' seminars have made investors focus more and more on the HMO market. And with good reason too; it is a growing market. I am not going to talk about 'No Money Down' because you will need some money. I will not talk about 'Passive income' either because you are going to have to set properties up and probably actively manage them.

Apart from students and professionals, there are also another raft of good earners and good payers. They may be factory workers for example (we have had a lot working at Amazon). Or they may be people from other trades such as the motor industry (there will always be cars of some type) hairdressers (most people will always have hair) funeral directors (no need to explain) then shared housing for students or professionals and now even more for 'DSS' (old terminology for people claiming state benefits) so the HMO strategy then is definitely here to stay. Lower costs to the tenants, lots of benefits, but with that comes more of us doing it. We need to stay ahead of the game.

More HMOs For Sale

With changing legislation and other changes in tax law there has been and will continue to be HMOs being put on the market by fed up landlords. Landlords who have done it for years, seen it all, had good income, but are now seeing it as a failing market because 'there are no students' or 'no one wants to share', actually, they do. But those landlords have not kept ahead, have not changed with the time and trends, have not updated, have not assessed the market properly. Doom and gloom merchants.

More opportunities for new HMO investors then.

Lovely new HMOs are coming on the market now all with mod cons, dressed, professionally photographed and ready to go. The old 'fuddy duddy' ones will not stand a chance and will get left behind. Expectations are for modern surroundings, cool areas to study, places to sit and chill, latest technology and entertainment (Netflix, superfast broadband, USB ports). Nice interiors, dressed beds, good mattresses, clean environments, maintenance done yesterday. It's just not like it was in the 'olden days' and if we can grasp that then we are onto a winner. There are lots of tired HMOs out there to be had by people with drive, imagination, flair and, hopefully, a business brain.

<Blank Page>

Chapter 3 - What HMOs Can Do for You

Do I need any money to start out?

Yes, you do.

This book will not talk about the 'No Money Down' deals that many trainers talk about. I have not come across one deal yet where no money is required. You may be able to do deals with other people's money (Joint Venture Finance for example or Angel Funding), but it is still money and you will have to pay it back or have an agreement to earn less. Nothing comes for nothing. The R2R strategy we talk about is low entry in terms of money up front. You will not own the asset (the property) but you will have control of the income it generates. You will need money to set up your business. No business can be set up without any money at all. But the plan is when you are up and running successfully, you can start paying yourself back.

How much income could I generate?

This is going to depend on how committed you are. You should be aiming to generate at least £500 per property per month on a R2R deal but this could be significantly higher if you buy and then you achieve a Return on your Investment (ROI).

For example, if you were to acquire SIX R2R deals over twelve months (very achievable) then you should be generating the following:

Profit of £500 per calendar month x 12 months

= Profit of £6,000 per annum

x 6 properties

= £36,000 PER ANNUM

This will of course but subject to HMRC tax, but you see the general picture. This income is greater than a teacher's salary who works full time in a stressful job. Running six properties will be a PART TIME job and significantly less stressful.

Training

Invest in yourself and your business. Be prepared for this investment or it could cost you dearly if you have not learned the fundamentals of property ownership and property management. People learn all the time for hobbies and are prepared to pay to learn so why shouldn't we do this for property when so much is at risk?

Learn on the job. Speak to other people who are doing it and offer to do some work with them for a while if you can, go along to viewings, go and look at properties with them, learn, learn, learn before you leap.

Planning and Finances

No business runs without a business plan. Have no plan and you are setting yourself up to fail from the outset. Find out what money you can access up front, be that from family, friends, loans (be careful) or even 0% credit cards. However, if you are borrowing, those borrowing costs must be factored into your deals, you must pay it back. You also need to plan how to pay it back if the deal goes wrong or have a Plan-B. For example, if you buy a property then struggle to find tenants for use as an HMO, you could then let it to a family, but will the figures still work without causing you financial difficulty?

Mindset

You may think this is dull or even obvious, but a lot of investors seem to miss this out when they are planning their business. It is important that you understand some fundamental mindset rules before you get going. You also need to have it clear in your mind about what this is not, and it is not a 'get rich quick' scheme. There will be hard work and dedication, it goes with any business and you should be prepared for that. But overall, this WILL succeed if you have the right approach and do something every day that takes you nearer your long-term goal. You may want a property to achieve cashflow and nothing else. You may decide you want cashflow and a long-term investment for capital appreciation which is what I talked about in my introduction. Either way, you need a plan, you need a strategy, write it down. Work out what it is you need to get going and a plan of how you will get from A to B.

Not everything in life goes 100% to plan and property investing has its highs and lows like anything else. Things will go wrong, people will let you down, but if you put the necessary steps in place to reduce risk you will be ok.

Number Crunching

In my area (and mine is not that different from anywhere else although it is Article 4 – which we will cover later), in comparison to a regular family let, the figures for an HMO let can be quite astonishing.

There are some variables of course, the mortgage rate has been assumed at 5% and the rents £350 per room on the HMO, the bills could be higher due to overuse and needs to be managed properly but even with the scenario above there is still a little bit of 'wiggle room' for that reason, and there is still double the profit of a single family let.

	Family Let	HMO Let
Property	3-Bed House	3-Bed house with 4x rooms
Purchase Price	£ 120,000	£ 120,000
Rental Amount	£ 700 pcm	£ 1,400 pcm
Mortgage	£ 375 pcm	£ 375 pcm
Less: Bills	-NA-	£ 300 pcm
Profit	£ 325 pcm	£ 725 pcm

HOWEVER, with increased income comes increased risk. That is not just property or HMOs, that is the way the world works. Family lets are USUALLY (not always), lower risk, little 'bother' and tend to run themselves if you have good tenants. HMOs are HARDER WORK as you have FOUR or more people to deal with who very often, DON'T COMMUNICATE with each other, so you end up having more than one conversation about the same thing. But if you know that and particularly if you enjoy interaction with people, do not let it worry you. Just know it is harder work. If you are wanting an increased income from property, be prepared to spend more time on it.

HMOs are good at providing a SECOND income. I would never recommend leaving the day job until you have this under your hat. You would need quite a few HMOs to get to the point of enough income to be able to leave your job

– THOUGH IT IS POSSIBLE. If you can do this part time or perhaps if there is a stay at home parent, this can fit nicely into a family routine and provide extra income, I know I have done it. You also need to figure out 'out of hours' calls if you have children tucked up in bed.

Like most things there are solutions to most problems you could come across and the aim of this book is to help you work through what being an HMO landlord could throw at you. We have done it; we have your back.

If you are about to embark on this HMO journey all I ask is that you treat this as a business with all the ups and downs of business, the risks and the pitfalls and if you can get it all running smoothly you will reap good, constant cashflow from them.

CHAPTER 4 - LET'S OPEN A GYM

I wanted to show you how this HMO business really is just that, a BUSINESS. Sadly, some property people do not see it like that. They see it as a 'side line' , a 'passive income' on the side (it's not passive unless you don't have to work at it), or even a hobby to build up some extra cash for the things they need and become 'financially free'.

Now imagine you are going to do a completely different BUSINESS, what would you need to DO to get your new gym up and running and do it profitably so it makes a good reliable income month after month. You want to have good happy (and fit) customers, recommending you to their friends....

Here is what you would do hopefully. For ANY business

- ✓ Where should the gym be located based on demographics?
- ✓ What do you want to be paying for the building rental? Or should you purchase?
- ✓ What equipment should you have, and do you buy second hand or new?
- ✓ What are the legal requirements for running a gym?
- ✓ Who will run it and how many hours should you dedicate to the gym?

- ✓ Pricing – how much do you charge? What do your competitors charge?
- ✓ Why would they come to your gym as opposed to another local gym, what makes yours stand out?
- ✓ What will go in there, how it will look, what will be ambience be, do you have music playing (you might need a licence to play music).
- ✓ Refreshments
- ✓ Vending machines
- ✓ Equipment maintenance
- ✓ Building maintenance
- ✓ Cleaning
- ✓ Should you belong to any regulatory bodies?
- ✓ Should you offer any extras for free, to get people in?
- ✓ How do you deal with complaints?
- ✓ How do you get feedback?
- ✓ How do you grow your business when this one is successful?
- ✓ How much money do you need up front? Where do you get it from?
- ✓ Do you know everything you need to know, or should you 'YouTube' what you do not?

So, I think you get the general idea. Running property is most definitely a BUSINESS and you need to be in the mindset of it being one, otherwise things can go drastically wrong, your business will not make the money you dream of, it will be sinking you into a hole in the ground with lots of debt too.

<Blank Page>

Chapter 5 - Knowing Your Strategy

Strategy Option One: Buy-to-Let

Some of you reading this will already know the direction you want to go as a lot will depend on the finance you have available. If you have enough to cover a deposit to purchase, then maybe that is the right way for you. But buying any Buy-to-Let is risky unless you have done your due diligence and I hope this book will help you do that. Financially you will need 25% of the purchase price as deposit, in addition you will need legal fees (normally around £1,200 if straight forward) and stamp duty which is charged on a sliding scale and you can find out about this at https://www.gov.uk/stamp-duty-land-tax/residential-property-rates

If you can find a property you can convert to an HMO, you may be able to RE-FINANCE the property after it is let and tenanted. This is complex and will depend on what you spend on it, how much you must 'develop' it and how large it is. A decent mortgage adviser is a good starting point. You will of course have to pay for revaluation. Always use a specialist HMO Mortgage adviser who can access 'whole of market'. Make sure you ask if they can.

Types of Mortgage

FIXED RATE mortgages give certainty about the amount your payment will be for a fixed period before it reverts to the variable rate. So, this is handy for financial planning. You may pay more for a fixed rate, but it means you do not have to cringe when you hear in the news that the Bank of England is putting up the base rate. Yours will not go up until the fixed term ends

VARIABLE RATE mortgages are a bit riskier but can also save you money as variable rates CAN BE lower than the fixed rates. But of course, your payments can swing right down and right UP again if interest rates change.

INTEREST ONLY mortgages are the most common types of mortgage for investors who do Buy-to-Let whether single lets or HMO. Very often lenders will want to know if you have any experience of managing property if you apply for a mortgage for an HMO and if you have not then you may find borrowing more difficult. With this type of mortgage, you will NOT reduce the capital you borrowed on the property, you will literally just be paying interest and you will still owe the same at the end of the term.

Strategy Option Two: R2R

Others will have fewer funds available for deposits and therefore will have chosen the R2R strategy where you 'rent' a property from an owner and then by their agreement, you are able to let the rooms out one by one to single occupants, following all the HMO licensing conditions or regulations. You agree to pay the owner regardless of whether you have no people in it or it is full.

That is your risk. Which is why again you must do 'Due Diligence'.

It is crucial that you have all costs up front considered for you to do your 'Deal Analysis'. You can get already done 'Deal Analysis' templates, but I find they work better for me if I have made mine to suit how I work. Keep it simple, list all your outgoings on one sheet then list your income on the other side and see if you have a profit/loss at the end. You must be truthful in what you put, you are only kidding yourself, no one else if you hide things that need to go in there.

<Blank Page>

Chapter 6 – Legalities of HMOs

Legal Definition of an HMO

This is a Housing Act classification for a house (or flat) with 3 or more occupants, forming 2 or more households

For example, a 2-bed flat with a couple and an unrelated friend in the 'spare' room would be an HMO and subject to HMO regulations

ARTICLE 4 (PLANNING)

Just by way of an explanation, some Local Authorities have removed permitted development rights of normal family houses that are to be turned into HMOs. In those areas before regulation, you could just get on with it. If the Council has imposed its Article 4 direction it means they do not generally want any more HMOs in the area and will certainly put a cap on new HMOs coming on stream. Why? In 2008 the Government wrote a report about 'Studentification' of some major towns and cities by students who were seen to cause blight on the areas and inflict anti-social behaviour. All a lot of old nonsense really as I have seen more Council housing areas that are far more deprived and have many anti sociable tenants living in them.

LICENSING (AMENITY STANDARDS)

I am going to mention this now as it is continuously mixed up with the Planning side of things and Article 4 that I have mentioned above. Licensing is NOTHING to do with Planning. And in fact, they are covered by TWO different Council departments who do not always speak to each other. You can have a house that has a licence granted but has NO planning permission to even exist. Similarly, you could have a house with full planning permission but NO licence. You must have BOTH. But in an area that does not have this permitted development taken away, you do not need to apply for planning permission its already 'granted' there is no need to ask for it.

Quite simply Licensing is about what is INSIDE the property – amenities, standard of repair, heating, enough facilities, fire detection and fire escape

Article 4 is to do with PLANNING and without planning permission you cannot operate an HMO.

You need to distinguish these two apart. I have known even Surveyors and Solicitors get this wrong.

LICENSING (FIT AND PROPER PERSON)

In addition to meeting the Council's amenity standards for HMO Licensing, the council will want to be sure that the property manager is a 'fit and proper person' and as such will have to confirm that they have no unspent convictions (not necessarily housing related) and have had no civil penalties for housing related matters.

ANYONE WHO OPERATES A R2R PROPERTY WHICH REQUIRES A LICENCE MUST HAVE THEIR NAMES ADDED TO THAT LICENCE – IT IS AN OFFENCE NOT TO DO SO.

FOUR BEDROOMED HMOS (NOT REQUIRING A LICENCE)

These types of HMO are extremely popular because generally they do not require a licence to run them. Here are some tips:

- ✓ Never let more than four people occupy or you will need a licence and you could be fined for not having one.
- ✓ Make sure you follow the council's amenity standards on their website for non-licensable HMOs. I would recommend however that you make your smaller HMO compliant to HMO licence standards as rules can change and you may need to license in the future.
- ✓ Make sure all rooms are minimum 6.51 square meters for a single person occupancy.
- ✓ Always ask the council to do an inspection once finished (or before) to make sure it complies to their standards.

- ✓ The minimum requirements will be a fire door on the kitchen, heat sensor in the kitchen, thumb turn locks on all exits, a fire blanket in the kitchen, wall mounted and smoke alarms in all bedrooms and circulation space. For more information use this link and download https://www.dashservices.org.uk/resources/fire-safety/document-2
- ✓ If you let on individual tenancies (not group) you must follow the guidance for 'bedsits'.
- ✓ It may be that some windows may need to be changed for fire escape reasons which is why it is important you read this document from the outset.

BUILDING REGULATIONS

Building regulations are minimum standards for design, construction and alterations to virtually every building to ensure health and safety. They are developed by the Government and overseen by Local Council Building Control. Building regulations do not only apply to large building projects but also to improvements and alterations such as new boiler systems, new windows, replacing fuse boards. You will need to check with your local council if you need to do any significant improvements or alterations. More information can be found at www.planningportal.gov.uk.

Chapter 7 – Finding Your Dream HMO

What you must remember is that YOU are not going to be living in it. You should be in the mindset of your 'customer' who may be a student or young professional, possibly without transport and who wants to be as near as possible to the city. If it is not a road you would live in, it does not mean that some of these people will not. If it is a popular area for HMOs and there is not lots of crime and anti-social behaviour you should be ok.

Location

- ✓ Look in areas of reasonably high density of HMOs as those areas should work. Oversaturation may be a problem, make sure the other HMOs are letting successfully.
- ✓ Look on www.spareroom.co.uk to see if there is an oversupply or an undersupply of HMOs by looking at rooms wanted/rooms offered ratios
- ✓ Make sure it is near to city and walkable. Students especially, will not walk.
- ✓ Try and have at least one parking space if possible. If you need to apply for planning, parking spaces are essential, and councils operate a parking per person ratio so you must ask.

- ✓ Try university cities but call the university accommodation office and talk about demand areas. Usually they are quite honest.
- ✓ Talk to the council about demand areas, they too can be quite helpful. You will need to speak to environmental health and planning
- ✓ Is the property in an Article 4 area? These areas are local authority areas where making a new HMO is pretty much a no-go. It depends on HMO/family ratio but get this wrong and you will be in breach of planning law. Ask the planning dept. Also, you could find out on the local Council's website if you do a search on 'HMO' or 'Article 4' etc.
- ✓ For R2R, do not take on an HMO which has been standing empty for some time and has been put on the R2R market in desperation. The base rent may be unrealistically high, and the figures will not work. Consider how much the house would be if it were normal family let. That will indicate whether the price has been over-inflated as it's set up as an HMO. It may be empty for a reason.
- ✓ What is the area like at night? Do a 'drive by' in the darker hours
- ✓ Get some local knowledge; there is loads of it about. I nearly bought a house that had a massive right of way

issue and I only found out by asking local shop owners. It would have been a total nightmare. Ask locals; they will tell you what the area is like

- ✓ Join networking groups for that area. Go to them and speak to local landlords about the area in which you are thinking of investing
- ✓ Join networking groups online and ask questions about the area
- ✓ In my area one road can be a complete no-go (drug area etc) and a few roads the other way might work fine, it can just depend on the road itself
- ✓ Look at the other houses, the neighbours' houses. Are there run down properties, lots of rubbish, graffiti, lots of dodgy looking people around?
- ✓ Ask the police. Very often you can get local crime info online its useful. Visit www.police.uk and enter the postcode for a crime summary of the area
- ✓ Talk to specialist HMO Letting Agents. They are quite hard to find but if you do find one that says 'yes we do let HMOs' then there is a whole plethora of other important questions you need to ask to see if they are telling the truth. If they are telling the truth they are likely to know demand areas and whether a certain road should let. I tried this recently in Telford and I do not know the area

that well (though I do not live too far away). The guy in the agency who I know, told me what to avoid and what to go for, he was helpful. This was mainly because I said that I wanted to work with them to help me let them. Win-win. They usually are honest (though not always) as they will not want to take on a load of hassle if they know they can't let the rooms

- ✓ Upcoming Article 4 areas (soon to be all of Birmingham and Coventry to name two) are good areas to invest in as it is likely that up and running HMOs will increase the property value when there is a blanket 'no more HMOs' in that area. This is good news for R2Rs as it is a good negotiating tool (rent me your house and your house value will go up) or for people investing to make some instant equity
- ✓ Some areas have additional licensing which covers all properties, not just HMOs so it is always best just to check on the Local Council's website
- ✓ Choose an area you can get to easily. If you must get there in a hurry (especially if self-managing) then it is not ideal to be travelling miles at night, for example, because someone is locked out
- ✓ Some areas just outside Article 4 areas really work. Look at the immediate roads next to the Article 4 areas. For

example, in Wolverhampton, there is Willenhall which is just over the border but in Walsall Council area where there is high demand but no Article 4 restriction.

The Power of Networking

There are lots of reasons to network, but the main reason must be 'getting your name out there' and letting people know what you do. For those of you wishing to find properties to buy or rent then you need to be in front of an audience full of either landlords or Letting/Estate agents.

Let's be honest, not everyone likes doing it as we can find it outside of our comfort zone, but I can assure you that once you have been to a few (and you could go with someone you know to your first one) then you will want to go networking all over the place.

- ✓ Make yourself go to at least one networking event per month
- ✓ When you go make sure you talk to or engage with at least three people as your initial target
- ✓ Take your business cards
- ✓ You will be surprised what you know, what you can pass on and who you know. These connections are key
- ✓ Leverage other people's networks think how many people they know.

- ✓ Go to the right networks, if you are looking for property then do not just go exclusively to events where there are other investors, you need to go to landlord events too.
- ✓ You can network and learn on training events for landlords
- ✓ Keep it going if you find a good one, people get to know you and even look for you if you are not there.
- ✓ Join their network community online so you can continue connections when the event is not running
- ✓ Have a prepared pitch, very often the event asks for people to stand up and say who they are and what business they are looking for. Know what connections you are looking for
- ✓ You might be able to find connections in advance of the meeting online; make sure you go and say 'hi'

Property Types

For operating HMOs, you nearly ALWAYS need to find houses, this is because flats generally just are not big enough and can bring in their own problems if let as HMO (noise etc). It can work possibly say if there is a shop underneath. But you will need to make sure that it is big enough. So:

- ✓ Houses - not flats

- ✓ The average HMO will be a house that has minimum three bedrooms and two reception rooms enabling four or more occupants
- ✓ Anything over four people occupying (not tenants) will need a licence as that is a legal requirement.
- ✓ The licence rule for it being more than two storeys was removed in 2018. You need a licence for anything with more than four occupants, as standard across the UK
- ✓ Each room for a bedroom needs to be 6.51sq meters. Anything under this is not lettable if you need a licence for it. If it does not require a licence (so four occupants or under) we still recommend 6.51sq in case the licence rules change and you need one in future, particularly if you are buying. If there is no communal space, the minimum room size will increase (i.e. >6.51 sq. m).
- ✓ For 'R2R' put a break clause in your contract which will enable you to end contract should licence rules change, and you find you cannot let some of your rooms
- ✓ If your kitchen has a dining kitchen so big enough for tenants to eat in, with somewhere to sit, you can potentially use your second reception room as a bedroom. However, you must have some dining space as you could fail under HHSRS risk assessment should the council become involved. We will cover this later in the book

- ✓ Have a property that does not require loads of updating. Do not promise new kitchens and bathrooms etc unless you have significantly reduced your rent to your landlord. You would be improving their asset not yours.
- ✓ Choose your property from the point of view of your 'customer' and how it's going to work as a multi let. And if you had to live there, would you? Could you?
- ✓ Live in your HMO for one night when finished, you may find all sorts of things that are irritating (sockets or furniture in wrong place etc) or things that don't work. Make it fun, take the kids, have a 'camp out' before anyone moves in. Get feedback from your sleepover buddies.

CHAPTER 8 - CONSIDERING COSTS

R2R Costs

- Fees to agent (they are still chargeable despite the fee ban as you are not a 'tenant')
- Deposit up front – you may be able to negotiate this down or have it removed immediately as you are guaranteeing the rent. This is likely to be the same as a month's rent. Add it in, you can always take it out
- Rent up front – try and get a month's rent free which is totally possible. Sign all the papers and pay the fees but before you do also negotiate a later start date after you have keys so you can start setting up. I know a lot of people who have achieved this – if you do not ask you do not get

Furniture

This will be a minimum £600 per room if not already furnished. It is a huge cost and is not factored in very well by investors. You may decide to have a loan or put stuff on an Argos card or other credit card etc, but you must factor in the repayments.

Furniture	Cost per Room
Wardrobe	£ 100
Chest of drawers	£ 60
Bedside table	£ 40
Bed base/frame	£ 120
Decent mattress	£ 120
Dressing items	£ 50
Desk	£ 60
Chair	£ 20
Total per Bedroom	**£ 570**

On top of this unless you can do it yourself you must think about transport/delivery costs and assembly. Do as much of it yourself as you can. If you are doing R2R, then possibly have a look at lease options for your furniture. That means you do not get left with loads of furniture you cannot store at the end of the lease (see below).

Add in the COMMUNAL AREAS so two nice Klippan sofas from Ikea which are roughly £ 200 each but are hardwearing and you can buy new covers quite cheaply, they are nice and funky colours and the added bonus is that you can get one of those in a standard car as they are self-assembly.

So, for a standard FOUR person HMO we are already up to £2,680. Then add in coffee tables, lamps, a TV (just a standard one), so probably £3,000 should about do it.

Add that into a standard three-year lease and you are looking at £1,000 per year or £83 per month (presuming 0% interest)

You can also find companies who do ASSET LEASING and will cover most of your set up costs like those above. And the costs are all TAX DEDUCTABLE

Other Costs

- ✓ **REFURBISHMENTS**: A whole subject in need of its own book.
- ✓ **INSURANCES**: For BTL you will need buildings insurance which must include public liability and your insurer must be aware you are doing an HMO. For R2R, you will also need public liability insurance – the owner's insurance is not enough and will not cover your liability to your tenants. It is a specialist insurance but is available
- ✓ **COMPLIANCE**: This is crucial, and we will cover it later. But you will need to consider fire doors and smoke alarms (hard wired in each room with battery back-up), heat sensor in kitchen (linked to main alarms), fire blanket in kitchen and thumb turn locks on all exits. You may even have to change some of the windows to 'escape' type windows

- ✓ **GAS AND ELECTRICITY**: Always do comparisons on a comparison website if you can and check your tariff. It is surprising how much you can shave off the monthly cost of your gas and electric consumption. It may be underestimated when you start out so be prepared for that if the property has not been an HMO before. Take advice from the utility company. I always take the figure of £ 35 per room for both and at least budget for that. Keep paying the same amount in the summer as you did in the winter to spread the costs. Invest in a 'Hive' system which you can regulate from an App but remember strictly speaking you should not control temperatures in an HMO, it is against the HHSRS Risk Assessment guidelines we will talk about later. Use the Hive if you really must (there is are other systems available).

- ✓ **WATER**: This will not alter each month unless the property has a meter. Check if it has because that could be costly if you have four or more people. A water meter once installed, cannot be taken out so you will need to think about that carefully. The water supplier should be able to give you an idea of costs based on a multi-let property

- ✓ **INTERNET**: This is probably the BIGGEST cause of complaint if it goes wrong so choose the supplier carefully. It can give you heaps of stress if it goes down or does not work properly. Personally, I have always used Virgin as you do not need a phone line for it to work and their customer services are good if something goes wrong. Have a good speed internet, chose cheap and you will quickly regret it

- ✓ **NETFLIX**: I have Netflix for my tenants which is relatively cheap, and four people can log on at any one time, so I use it at my own house as well. All the tenants are rarely on it together
- ✓ **TV LICENCE**: If you provide a TV you will need to buy a licence. However, if the tenants use their laptops to stream live TV in their rooms you need to tell them to buy a licence or they will have their collar felt by TV Licensing.

Using Contractors

Of course, in many circumstances you will be needing work done on your HMO whether that be minor cosmetic work on a R2R deal or larger building work on a BTL HMO you are renovating

In both cases you need to follow some golden rules, and, in all cases, you need to have written agreements about costings as things can go horribly wrong and there may be no recourse to recover your funds

- ✓ Always go for recommendations from your property network
- ✓ Have a look at work they have already done and get testimonials
- ✓ Meet them on site and make sure they have a full understanding of what is required before you take the property over, involve them in the process and this way they can tell you if they feel there is anything worrying about the property (damp etc)
- ✓ Get everything in writing on a proper letterhead. Make sure you have an address for your contractor in case anything goes wrong
- ✓ Agree stage payments, never the whole project up front. Release money for materials and ask them to hand over receipts (they may be putting a big mark-up on materials at your expense). If there is a dispute further down the line, they could take your materials off site with them
- ✓ Ask for copies of their insurance – public liability
- ✓ See if they are members of any trade associations
- ✓ Make sure building control pass off the work before you make the final payment

- ✓ Payment terms should be made between both parties in writing
- ✓ Agree a time schedule with penalty clauses for running over late as the project being completed late will cost you money.

Negotiating Your Deal

The art of doing any deal is within the negotiation. You need to keep your feet on the ground and in the excitement of starting off, it can be easy to make mistakes just to get your first deal 'over the line'. There are several useful strategies here to help.

R2R

With the R2R strategy, you can either going via an Agent or try to contact a landlord direct. There are plenty of 'tired' landlords out there wanting to offload. The older and more traditional landlords are likely to 'just give it to an agent', it is less hassle for them, and they do not have to do much.

Letting Agents

Firstly, you need to understand what it is like in the current Letting Agency business.

Having worked on the other side of the desk I can give a very honest take on this. To put it into context, Letting Agents have had a tough time lately especially with the Tenant Fee ban in 2019 coming into effect so tenants cannot be charged hardly ANY fees at all.

They see people who want to do R2R strategy as competitors and a threat. They fear that such investors want to take properties out of their portfolio, run them themselves for huge profits and never do any work with the agent again.

You need to turn all that around if YOU want to get THEM to offer you properties. So, to start, I am going to give you some real tips on what to say and what not to say.

Heed what I say, this will work.

You need to make this a win-win situation for BOTH you and the agent. Demonstrate to them that by you 'leasing' a house from them under this arrangement will not negatively affect them financially at all, in fact it could work to their advantage and make them more money. These are the things to remember, make note of them off and learn them so you are good to go for 'that conversation'.

- You are NOT taking a property from their portfolio; they will still be the main contact between you and the Landlord
- They can still charge you an ADMIN fee (do not offer this but be open to it if they mention it)
- You could potentially take a property off them that may not be renting out that well (as you can do some minor improvements)

- They will still get paid their LET FEE in the normal way should they have let the property to anyone else
- They will still be able to charge their % monthly management fee to the Landlord
- They still retain control and have the property in their portfolio and still have 'their' landlord
- You want an ONGOING working relationship with them, and they are very welcome to see what you have done when all ready to go as an HMO and you will want MORE property from them
- There will be NO VOIDS as you are taking the hit on those
- There will be NO RENT ARREARS as you are taking the risk on those too
- They will have LESS work to do because YOU are looking after the tenants, so they do not have to (callouts etc).

Isn't that now a win-win?

And please do not go into the agents talking about R2R HMOs on a Corporate basis' as a lot of them will not know what you are even talking about. Just explain that you want a house to take on so you can let the rooms out to professionals on an individual rental basis. Say something like 'you know, like a house share'. You will find that they will probably light up as they start to understand what you are talking about.

Once you have won the agent over by all this smooth-talk, have a guess how much easier the agent's job will be to convince the landlord? Most agents have very good working relationships with their landlords and an immense amount of trust builds up. I know that if I had put a proposition to a landlord that I was wholly 100% bought into (because of how it is put across) then most landlords would say 'if you think it's a good idea Marie, we will go along with it'.

Leave any ego at the door, all the stuff you might have been taught on the big 'free' courses, in most cases it doesn't' work and the agent will literally roll their eyes, they have heard it all before. Use this technique and I can guarantee you will get further. I have had mentees who have followed this, and they said how much easier it has been. It is relationship building and joint venture working with an agent. Now that sounds better does not it. It makes the whole thing so much less scary too because you are giving something back, not just taking it away.

So, now onto my advice:

- Letting Agents have a living to make, do not presume they are going to 'give stuff away' they are not. Be nice, be polite, do business with them which will make it a win-win for you, the agent and the landlord. It is a bit about approach and attitude. It is not all about you.

- Visit as many as you can personally, if your investment area is a drive away, plan a day when you go into as many as you can and repeat, on-masse.
- Try and find smaller, independent agents. Do this by finding them on' To Let' boards you don't recognise in your area (the type that possibly won't have an office) or the smaller 'corner shop' type agents usually in the middle of really good letting areas. You can then speak to the decision maker not someone on a desk
- Make your first good contact your best buddy. Connect with them, chat to them, get to know them. They are more likely to refer. Do not overdo it.
- Keep the momentum going, if you visit an agent and you feel it was positive even though they didn't have anything right now, go back, drop in, speak to the staff, build on relationships so if they do have a deal come in, you are in the front of their minds
- Network, go to network events oozing with Letting Agents, get to know them, buy them a coffee, polite handshake, business cards, connect on Facebook

- Never try to cut an agent out of a deal. Word spreads, just do not do it, its bad business and it will come back and bite you

- Ask for viewings out of hours, you might get in front of the landlord.

- Run a search on 'managing agents' in your area online, lots of them call themselves managing agents but are really 'Letting Agents' in disguise. Call them and ask them if they have anything that is proving hard to let.

Direct to Vendor

In my opinion this is trickier as you will not know where they live but you could give it a go, some people do very well out of it.

✓ Contact the council and ask them for a list of registered HMOs in your area they must release this under 'Freedom of Information'.

✓ Contact www.whatdotheyknow.co.uk which is an amazing Freedom of Information service to get pretty much anything you want from the council as long as it doesn't breach GDPR regulations. It might give you landlord home addresses, or it will just identify the HMO addresses for you. Write to them.

- ✓ When you write to a landlord many people use the personal approach and put the letters in attractive coloured envelopes and hand write on the front, it sometimes work if they are picking up a pile of unopened post, it will stick out

- ✓ Networking events. So many people try to find deals going to events where other investors are. Why? You need to be where landlords are. Find out from your council if they run regular landlord events, often they do. Or training courses for landlords. Go where landlords are. Builders merchants/plumbers/carpet shops/ironmongers. Put in a leaflet

- ✓ Social media network groups for property investors. Join them, join in the chat, do not always take, sometimes just answer posts. Get known

- ✓ If there isn't a network group for landlords in your area, make one. I did and I got loads of 'fed up' and moaning landlords desperate to sell their HMOs.

- ✓ Go onto www.spareroom.co.uk and find contact numbers of landlords who are letting, look for the shabby rooms and bare/undressed beds. Try and get those and turn them into lovely places to live. Some landlords just give up.

- ✓ Try www.openrent.co.uk where you can contact landlords directly. The message normally goes straight to them. Be persistent
- ✓ Put adverts in the local press (quite expensive but can work), also adverts in shop windows, people do look. Gumtree/Marketplace, all the usual places – remember to set up 'alerts' to your inbox when a new property comes up
- ✓ Stick a magnet on your car they are really cheap; 'HOUSES WANTED FOR GUARNTEED RENT' or if doing BTL then 'WE BUY HOUSES FOR CASH' etc.

Ready Let HMOs

If you can find one of these, you are onto a winner. No furniture costs, no let fees, just ready income as soon as you sign on the dotted line.

A few things to remember: all tenants will need to be served with a legal notice about change of landlord.

If the property is already an HMO but NOT tenanted, ask why it is empty; an empty HMO might just be empty because there is no demand.

Ask for copies of rent statements for at least the last 12 months and ask plenty of questions to see why it is not let.

Using Sourcing Agents

Another way of finding properties if you are short of time is to use a registered sourcing agent. You will have to pay for it but there can be cost off-sets which in turn will just mean you get on your property journey sooner rather than later.

- ✓ Always use a fully registered sourcing agent. They must have Anti Money Laundering (AML) registration, be a member of the Property Redress Scheme (PRS), Information Commissioners Office (ICO) registered and have professional indemnity insurance and you can ask for this information and be given it readily, if you aren't then walk away.

- ✓ Find agents who are ready to work 'for' you, not just show you what they have on offer, although they may just have the property you are looking for on their books already

- ✓ Sourcing agents know a lot of property people and that's how property seemingly drops into their laps. However, they will have done a lot of work to get to that point, they can and do earn their fees

- ✓ Fees are typically £3,000 for a BTL or a R2R. Fees will be higher if the deal is offering a higher % return

- ✓ Register with quite a few and get on mailing lists, most of them use Mailchimp

- ✓ Ask them what they have sourced already to give you an idea of how experienced they are
- ✓ Always do your own due diligence on a property. Just because you are paying a sourcing agent does not mean it is a good deal. Its industry expected that you will check for yourself that there is demand and figures will work. It does not mean they are conning you; they might just have not checked.
- ✓ A sourced property may not be compliant for HMO standards you need to do all those checks too
- ✓ You can still negotiate price via a sourcing agent
- ✓ As I have already said above, if you can get them to source you a ready-to-go HMO which might also be ready let, you have your fees covered as you will have saved a small fortune.
- ✓ They will commonly ask you for a % of the fee upfront at the offer stage and this is perfectly legal as long as you have checked their compliance.
- ✓ Check their terms and conditions to see in what circumstances you would be able to get a refund. Very often you cannot get a refund if you pull out, but they will refund if the survey fails.

Chapter 10 - Next Steps

Due Diligence

- ✓ Check the numbers work and the % return on your investment is right for you. If its significantly higher than the bank % then it cannot be a bad deal, but you should be looking at 10% and above for an HMO
- ✓ That the area is right for you. Do not have it so far away you cannot get to it, you are responsible for the property wherever you are or if you have an agent or not
- ✓ That there is enough demand – many HMOs are being offloaded where the demand has dropped. The reason may be genuine but there might be something you just do not know
- ✓ Check the sourcing agent's registration, always. Do not skip this even if you may know them and you don't like asking. It is what they are paid for. Certainly, do this before you hand over any money
- ✓ Check that the seller/landlord is legitimate and always do a land registry check to make sure they have the right to lease/sell the property (cost about £6.00)
- ✓ Make sure the landlord has adequate building insurance

- ✓ Make sure the landlord's insurer has given permission to do multi let.
- ✓ Make sure you have more than one exit strategy. If your target market does not work, what would you do with it? Family let? Social housing?
- ✓ Ask for confirmation that the landlord's lender is aware of the lease arrangements
- ✓ If there is any lease (i.e. on a flat) in place you must ensure that the managing agent (normally blocks of flats) has given permission for what they call 'subletting'

Negotiating Your Terms

This does not apply too much to BTL HMO as you do not have so many things to negotiate and agree on apart from the price. Run your numbers and remember to work them out like this:

WORKING OUT GROSS YIELD:

VALUE OF HOUSE	£ xxxxx.00	(1)
TOTAL YEARLY RENT IN	£ xxxx.00	(2)

DIVIDE (2) BY (1) AND MULTIPLY BY 100 TO FIND GROSS YIELD

Once you have this then you will have yields to compare each house so you can decide which property will give you the best % yield from that investment

Running Your Numbers

Money-In	Money-Out
Room 1	Mortgage @ 5%**
Room 2	Insurances
Room 3	Gas/Electric
Room 4	Water
Etc.	Internet
	Gardener
	Furniture lease or credit card
	Cleaner
	Maintenance / Replacements ***
	Management – 10% of Rental
	Voids – 10% of Rental ****

** do this above the standard fixed rate to give you some room for the rates going up, it is called a 'stress test'

*** maintenance at 10% is the 'norm' for any property you own

**** include voids at 10% and anything less than that is then a bonus on your balance sheet

- ✓ Negotiate the price of course, make sure you do your homework and compare to other HMO sales in the area
- ✓ Buy with tenants in situ if they are good tenants
- ✓ Ask for a copy of the rent account for the last 2 years to establish if you want to keep the tenants or if you need vacant possession

- ✓ Get vacant possession if you want to do a major refurbishment, you just cannot do that with tenants in situ; it won't work
- ✓ Make sure the seller gets the tenants out before sale, that is not your job
- ✓ If you take the tenants on, then you need to get certain legal paperwork done. This applies to R2R or purchase. Otherwise you will have a problem if you try to evict a tenant later
- ✓ Negotiate start date/completion. You cannot be unreasonable but at least have plenty of time to get organised
- ✓ Keep the same agent if they manage. It will be so much easier for you and the tenant as they will already have a relationship with them
- ✓ Try and get the furniture and any white goods left in, it will save you a lot of money
- ✓ If there are any obvious maintenance jobs you can negotiate this in with your price. I know a landlord who agreed to replace the boiler prior to sale.

Case Study - Wolverhampton Buy-to-Let Deal

This is a good example of an HMO BTL property, running at almost 100% occupancy and good cashflow: (it is self-managed by the landlord)

Expenditure (pcm)		Income (pcm)	
Mortgage	330	Room 1	360
Utilities	150	Room 2	340
Council Tax	96	Room 3	340
Water	26	Room 4	310
Wi-Fi	36		
Voids	0		
Management	0		
Total Outgoings	**638**	**Total Income**	**1,350**

R2R

There is so much you can negotiate on here to make sure your lease goes smoothly and that you have a deal that suits both parties.

RUN YOUR NUMBERS:

Money-In	Money-Out
Room 1	Rent to Landlord
Room 2	Insurances
Room 3	Gas/Electric
Room 4	Water
Etc.	Internet
	Gardener
	Furniture lease or credit card
	Cleaner
	Maintenance / Replacements
	Management – 10% of Rental
	Voids – 10% of Rental

From this you will be able to see if your deal is going to work or not. If the figures are tight or in the negative you certainly will have to negotiate your base rent to the landlord or walk away, unless you think you have underestimated the room rentals. Make sure your voids go in. Even the best Manager / Landlord / Agent has voids that's just how it is. These HMOs are rarely full for 365 days a year, so don't beat yourself up when you have one. Just make sure you account for it, so you have some 'slippage'.

Case Study - Nottingham R2R 'deal'

This deal was run by me as part of a mentorship. You can see clearly here that there is a LOSS in this deal even though it was going to be self-managed. Therefore, it is so worth doing your numbers. It is an eight bedroomed house.

OUTGOINGS		**POTENTIAL RENT IN**	
Rent to Landlord	2,700	Room 1	550
Council Tax	150	Room 2	550
Water	60	Room 3	500
Gas & Elec	280	Room 4	500
TV	13	Room 5	500
Internet	40	Room 6	475
Furniture (Loan)	135	Room 7	475
Management	0	Room 8	450
Void	400		
Maintenance	75		
Spare room Ads	29		
Cleaner	80		
Gardener	10		
Insurance	40		
Total Outgoings	**4,012**	**Total Income**	**4,000**

Case Study-Wolverhampton R2R Deal

Expenditure (pcm)		Income (pcm)	
Rent	500	Room 1	350
Utilities	150	Room 2	350
Council tax	96	Room 3	275
Water	26	Room 4	275
Wi-Fi	36		
Voids	0		
Management	0		
Total Outgoings	**808**	**Total Income**	**1,250**

Another example of a good R2R deal

- ✓ Negotiate on your rent. Everyone starts somewhere but you can negotiate downwards if you tell the landlord what they will be saving on. The current rent may not reflect the actual value. Run your numbers
- ✓ Tell the agent/landlord that they will be saving on maintenance because you will attend any minor things. Do not offer to do too much at this stage as this maintenance gets expensive over the year. Damages are of course your responsibility anyway
- ✓ Point out that the landlord will have no void risk as they are having guaranteed rent from you
- ✓ If there is any furniture in there make sure they leave it and, of course, white goods too as it will save you ££££

- ✓ Always negotiate a break clause as this will protect both yourself and the landlord if things go wrong. For example, if selective licensing is brought into the area, the property may not fit the minimum standards so a break clause will mean you can give it back.

- ✓ Negotiate your rent based on the condition of the property and try really hard not to agree to things you don't need, but rather to get the landlord to do it or pay a lower rent for the first 12 months or however long it may take to recoup your spend. For example, a tired bathroom may affect your letability but if you can refurbish it, do so, but at the landlord's expense

- ✓ Do not spend too much on someone else's asset unless you are recouping that outlay over the term of the lease, you will have added value to the house that is not yours.

- ✓ Remember that if you are converting a house to do R2R HMO then you will increase its value especially if Article 4 is due to be brought in. When Article 4 is imposed, HMO prices go up as supply falls. This is a good negotiating tool to use with your landlord.

- ✓ Your contract with the landlord is key too. Make sure you know who does what and what happens if there is a major fault. I had a R2R riddled with rising damp and a landlord

I could not contact. It happens, but best avoided if you can.

- ✓ If your landlord has several other properties then negotiate on those too, you never know what might happen.

Business Compliance

LEASE AGREEMENTS – R2R

If you are taking on a property as a 'R2R' deal, then you must get the paperwork right. You cannot operate on an ASSURED SHORTHOLD TENANCY as you are not the tenant. 'ASTs' are only to be issued to individuals, not companies (but companies can use AST's to their tenants). If the Letting Agent or landlord does not have a lease agreement/Company Let agreement, then you can provide one for them. This makes their job easier. It is a much simpler process for them than letting to a tenant and there is a lot less compliance to follow for them. Copies of Lease agreements are available online and usually someone in your network will give you a copy of theirs if you ask. This is where networking and meeting people really pays off, most HMO Comrades will be very helpful. But do not just take, you must be prepared to give back to the 'community'. And remember to have it checked by a solicitor if you are unsure.

INSURANCE

You must of course have adequate insurance for any property you take on through whichever route. Find an insurer who is well versed with what the industry standard is and what cover you will require. With R2R deals, make sure that the owner has adequate buildings insurance and ask for copies; you cannot operate without it. The owner must also make sure his insurer has given permission for it to be let as an HMO. Make sure that you have adequate LEGAL cover which will also offer protection if you have a problem with a claim against you or the council try to fine you for any Health and Safety breaches. For standard BTL then you must do the same and have it insured from the time you take over the keys, also covering any time the property is standing empty and there can be restrictions on how long this can be. Always ask.

You are operating a business and it should be insured as one. You must obtain PROFESSIONAL INDEMNITY insurance in case someone tries to sue you. This could be the landlord making a claim for some kind of loss. For example, if she/he requires the property back and you cannot evict the tenants. Also insure for PUBLIC LIABILITY on each property in case there is a claim against a tenant. Both insurances are an absolute MUST. Your network will have recommendations.

DATA PROTECTION

This is now called GDPR. It is now a legal requirement that you register with the Information Commissioner's Office (ICO) prior to taking any information from prospective tenants. You must know how to store that information securely and know who you can/cannot give that information to. Breaches of GDPR can lead to big fines.

PROPERTY REDRESS SCHEME (PRS)

You are required to be part of this scheme if you are MANAGING tenants. It is an 'Ombudsman' scheme for tenants, so they have somewhere to go to raise a complaint against you or your company. You are not required to register if you buy your own property and rent it out to your tenants. However, this is subject to change. At the time of writing if you operate a R2R property you are required to register as you are a 'manager'. It is a formal complaint system and remember that if there is a valid complaint against your business you can have your registration removed and you would not be able to trade. 'Agents' who do not register can be investigated by Trading Standards.

Chapter 11 - Finding Tenants

Although this is not rocket science, there is still quite an art to finding good paying tenants and people who will mix well together, because not everybody does.

Tenant Types

PROFESSIONALS

These types of people are typically in well paid professions, may be post-graduates and will prefer probably something different to normal shared 'student type' houses. They may be in better paying jobs and can afford a bit more luxury for example en-suite rooms, so they do not have to share bathrooms. They may be accountants, in the legal profession, doctors, nurses etc

STUDENTS

A lot of landlords have historically been against housing students, but I am not sure why. Most of them are now on student finance and have mum/dad/family members as guarantors. Also, it is likely they will pay 'termly' and book as a group, although the latter is a bit less common now. They will usually pay and stay for a whole year although they may want a deal on their rent over the summer if they are not living in it. First years generally go into Halls, so you are likely to get more seasoned students living in houses and they are more likely to know how to run a hoover or washing machine.

'BLUE COLLAR' WORKERS

A bit of an old- fashioned name now but these group of people are more likely to work in factories, Amazon, be couriers, taxi drivers etc. It could be that they are transient and move jobs quite frequently so like the idea of shorter term and more flexible room rentals than a whole property. They are usually single and for no obvious reason are very often male.

HOUSING BENEFIT or 'DSS' TENANTS

The term 'DSS' is now totally outdated as the 'Department of Social Security' disappeared years ago. These tenants will rely on what is now Universal Credit where all their benefits are paid in one lump sum and they must manage their own money. The rent element usually is paid directly to the claimant not the landlord. People on Universal Credit can often swap into full-time work and vice versa. Their payment will strictly be the 'rent' element only and not the utilities and you will be asked for a breakdown and you will have to collect a 'top up' from the tenant each month to cover the shortfall.

You need to be very honest with your mortgage provider and your insurer about which tenant type will be living in your property as some may attract a higher rate or be totally refused. Additionally, your insurance might be invalid which would make you in breach of your mortgage terms anyway

Attracting Tenants

- ✓ MOST PEOPLE USE www.spareroom.co.uk but there are other portals such as Open Rent, Marketplace, Rightmove and Zoopla
- ✓ Make sure your advert looks excellent and stands out. Importantly keep it up to date and 'boost' your ad frequently (you may have to pay a bit extra)
- ✓ Dress your rooms, never advertise a room that has an undressed bed and a few nice things in the room, lamp, rug, pictures etc
- ✓ Take good photos in daylight on a good camera, get lots of angles of the room, people usually want to see all of it not just the bed. You can also add videos to some portals which is much better for people who cannot view because they may not be local
- ✓ Make a 'show room' as soon as you have the keys so you can get it advertised quickly. Be sure not to misrepresent

and if you are using other people's photos of how it is going to look, be honest and say that in your advert

- ✓ Be open to the idea of no deposit, see if you can get a guarantor instead
- ✓ Offer some incentives, gift vouchers, hamper, free week etc
- ✓ Think of some extras like 'Netflix' which is relatively cheap and might give you an edge over competitors
- ✓ Make sure your room rates are competitive
- ✓ Work the system, message advertisers, do not just wait for them to come to you
- ✓ Answer your ads quickly, the emails should come to your phone, people will not wait days for a reply
- ✓ Be available to do viewings quite quickly
- ✓ Arrive at the property early and put the heating on and tidy up
- ✓ Pick a good housemate to be 'around' to introduce themselves. Moving to a new home where other people live can be scary, it is good to know who you will be sharing with. Pay them in treats/vouchers

- ✓ Make sure your tenants are going to mix, for example someone on shifts may complain if others are up and about when they are trying to sleep.

Using Letting Agents

Many investors who do not live in their investment area use Letting Agents to let out and manage their HMOs. There is nothing wrong with that if you know that they are fully competent and compliant. Choose the wrong agent and you could find you have high voids or bad tenants. Very often if you are asking for a 'Let Only', they can take your money and run and leave you with a bad, disruptive and/or non-paying tenant.

There are some golden rules about finding a good agent to let your HMO, always ask the following questions.

COMPLIANCE: Are they registered with all the legally required bodies? There are PRS (Ombudsman), ICO (Data Protection), Client Money Protection. Do they have adequate professional indemnity insurance? You can ask to see all these documents and with the PRS you can call them and check your agent is registered. Some unscrupulous agents who are not registered or who have been banned, still use the logos but are not members.

EXPERIENCE: Have they managed HMOs before? If so, have they got HMOs now, where are they, numbers etc? Talk to the Letting Agents about how they find their HMOs are to manage and really get to understand how they do it. Do not just speak to the person on reception, there is too much risk to get this wrong

INSPECTIONS: How often? What do they check? Most importantly how do they feedback to you. You need to make sure they are checking all the areas that you could be fined 30k for.

DEPOSITS: What scheme does the agent use and how do they ensure that the deposits are lodged in time? If this is done correctly, the agent will not be able to serve section 21 if they fall into arrears or there are other breaches

MAINTENANCE: Find out what their procedure is for dealing with a) emergencies and b) routine maintenance. Try and do as much of it yourself or via your own tradespeople as they will charge an additional % on top of the contractor rate

RENT ARREARS: What is their arrears procedure and how soon do they tell you when someone has defaulted and how do they deal with it. At which point do they start legal action?

LICENSING: A really good one to 'test' your agents' knowledge. If they are experienced in HMOs, they will know the answer to this. So, you could ask them a 'test' question for example "Do I need to get a licence?" and see if they know the answer

TENANT RELATIONSHIPS: How do they deal with them and what reporting procedures are in place? Happy tenants = long term tenants

TENANT BREACH OF CONTRACT: What will they do if someone wants to leave early or just leaves early? What will they do to chase that tenant for keys/rent?

AND FINALLY: Make sure all of this and more is in a very tight well checked management agreement. Know your terms, check what is in it and if in doubt, seek advice. You may also be able to alter it to your requirements

At the time of writing, the Government is bringing in new legislation to make sure any Managing agent or Letting Agent take further training and an exam. This is called the Regulation of Property Agents (ROPA).

<Blank Page>

CHAPTER 12 - COMPLIANCE

Even if you are using an agent, you need to learn this because you must make sure they are doing it correctly. If they do not then you could end up with a bad tenant, you cannot get rid of. Therefore, it is so important you check they have Professional Indemnity too because if they give you a duff tenant there is some recourse and so too with the PRS if they are not doing things correctly.

Below are the things they (or you) MUST do at the start of the tenancy. This enables you to be able to start proceedings should you need to

A PROPER VALID TENANCY AGREEMENT: Ask to see a copy of the agreement they issue as it should have prescribed information on there, including name and address of where notices should be served. If it is a Let Only, your details must be on there

A VALID GAS CERTIFICATE: Must be issued at the start of the tenancy, a copy is fine. The tenant must sign for it otherwise you cannot prove they had it

RIGHT TO RENT: The agent must check the tenant's right to rent in this country and a valid passport or visa must be produced and checked. This applies to all tenants, not just people from overseas. There is much more information about this online and you need to know that they are entitled to live in this country, or you can be fined. The agent, or you, must take a copy of these documents. If an overseas tenant's visa runs out mid tenancy you must make sure you get an up to date one otherwise, they can be asked to leave the property/country.

HOW TO RENT BOOKLET: This must be issued and signed for and it must be the latest up to date copy hence I will not put the link on here. If you google 'How to Rent' booklet (make sure it is the government website) that is the one that is required. No booklet, no possession of the property should you need it, be warned

VALID EPC CERTIFICATE (See Property (HMO) Compliance): An EPC (Energy Performance Certificate) is the energy rating of the property and assessments must be done very 10 years. These can be obtained online from the EPC register using the property address and postcode and they are public record; anyone can access them. If there is no EPC provided and signed for, then no possession

DEPOSITS: Any deposit taken must be registered with an approved scheme within a certain timeframe. We will go much more into this in my next book. However, know that there are timescales and that prescribed information must be issued within timescales too. If that is not done properly, possession of the property will fail

Property (HMO) Compliance

We have talked a lot about business compliance and what agents and landlords need to be aware of but that is just the start. The property itself is going to have to meet strict criteria for it to be used as an HMO. Failure to meet the criteria could well lead to BIG council fines which can be up to £30,000 PER OFFENCE

The main things are going to be fire detection and escape and compliance with HHSRS (Housing Health and Safety Rating System).

GAS SAFETY: You must ensure that the boiler in the property is safe and that it has been maintained and tested properly each year. You should ask for copies of the certification when you take on the property

ELECTRICAL SAFETY: Each property must have been fully checked and tested by a qualified electrical engineer within the last five years. Additionally, you must do visual checks each time a tenant moves out to ensure all is well (cracked sockets, loose wires etc). It should also be part of your routine inspection regime. Ask to see certificates

EPC: Each property must have an up to date ENERGY PERFORMANCE CERTIFICATE which is valid for ten years. Properties with energy ratings lower than E will not be able to be let from June 2020

PORTABLE APPLIANCE TESTING: This is a requirement of a licensed HMO; however, I always recommend it is done in all HMOs to ensure any 'portable' equipment is safe: fridges, freezers, TV's, vacuum cleaners, microwaves, kettles etc. Anything bought in by the tenant does not have to be tested in this manner

MEANS OF ESCAPE FROM FIRE: This is massively important and is dealt with differently in each Local Authority area. LACORS and HOMESTAMP are normally the standards adopted for smaller HMOs that are not subject to mandatory licensing. These documents will tell you which guidance to follow for the different type of layout you may have. For example, you will be required to have easy exit locks on all doors, both external and bedroom doors. You will not be allowed to use a lock where a tenant will need a key to get out of the house or room safely.

Fire doors will also be required but the number and location will depend on your property layout.

EARLY FIRE DETECTION: This will include smoke alarms, hardwired into your main electrical circuit and they will all go off when someone burns the toast. This happens and is normal and necessary. Tenants should be taught about how to cook sensibly and open windows etc. The type of fire detection system will depend on your layout and again reference should be made to LACORS and HOMESTAMP as guidance.

ALWAYS SEEK THE ADVICE OF THE LOCAL AUTHORITY IF IN DOUBT, NEVER RISK A GOOD GUESS. THEY WILL COME OUT AND SEE THE PROPERTY OR OFFER ADVICE OVER THE PHONE

HHSRS (Housing Health & Safety Rating System)

There are 29 different categories of Hazard that the council will use to assess whether the property is compliant to these standards that they use on ANY property and HMOs are no different. If they decide to check your property, they will get this checklist out and use it. They are obliged to check for EVERY hazard, not just one that may have been complained about. Here are the main 'hazards'

HYGROTHERMAL CONDITIONS – damp and mould growth, excess cold, excess heat

POLLUTANTS – asbestos, biocides, carbon monoxide and fuel combustion products, lead, radiation, un-combusted fuel gas, volatile organic compounds

SPACE, SECURITY LIGHT AND NOISE – crowding and space, entry by intruders, lighting, noise

HYGIENE, SANITATION AND WATER SUPPLY – domestic hygiene, pests and refuse, food safety, personal hygiene, sanitation and drainage, water supply for domestic use

FALLS – falls associated with baths etc, falls on the level, falls associated with steps and stairs, falls between levels

ELECTRIC SHOCK, FIRES, BURNS AND SCALDS – electrical hazards, fire, hot surfaces and materials

COLLISIONS CUTS AND STRAINS – collision and entrapment, explosions, ergonomics, structural collapse and falling elements

THE HHSRS STANDARDS WILL ALSO INCLUDE MINIMUM ROOM SIZES. IF YOU GET THESE WRONG, YOU MAY HAVE ROOMS IN YOUR HMO THAT YOU CANNOT LET.

Penalties Under HHSRS

There are several ways that a Local Authority can treat a person who has received a notice for failures under the above HHSRS system. These range from an informal letter through to Rent Repayment Orders and Civil Penalties. We will go much more into this in my next book on Management, but you need to be aware that the property you are taking on does comply to certain minimum standards

LACORS & HOMESTAMP

In addition to the above each council will have its own AMENITY STANDARDS for HMOs and very often they are published on their website. If not, then you must ask for them as they will tell you what you need to do to be HMO Compliant. Both LACORS and HOMESTAMP are documents written by experts and endorsed by most Local Authorities and identify the standards that the property must have to comply with fire safety

Management Regulations

These are the main regulations that you or your managing agent MUST adopt because if they are not adhered to, fines of up to £30,000 can apply for any breaches:

The regulations impose duties on managers of HMOs to:

- Provide contact details to each household and have them on display
- Ensure that all means of escape from fire are maintained and kept free from obstruction, all fire precautions are maintained and that steps are taken to protect occupants from injury
- Maintain water supply and drainage
- Ensure annual gas safety checks are carried out, and electrical installations are checked every five years, and the manager must not unreasonably cause any interruption to gas or electricity supply
- Maintain in repair and keep clean all common parts and installations, and ensure common parts have adequate lighting
- Ensure each unit and furniture are clean at the start of each occupation and maintain the internal structure and installations in each letting
- Provide adequate waste storage facilities and ensure that there is appropriate collection of waste.

I will go into a lot more details about the Management Regulations and give you help with compliance in my next book about Managing HMOs

Avoiding Fines

Whilst many of the fines are related to Management, I will identify here some ways to avoid fines that will help you when you are setting up your HMO. My second book will tell you a lot more about running tenancies and your property compliantly

- ✓ Always engage with your local council, do not avoid them. Use them and call them into your property if in doubt, it is always better to be on the radar than under it
- ✓ Register with their local accreditation scheme which most councils have for 'good landlords'. This way they will come out and usually give you a star rating or at least a piece of paper or certificate to prove you have done everything correctly
- ✓ Be aware of your obligations, keep your training up to date and attend landlord events in your area, be ahead of the game. A lot of training events can give you CPD points (Continuous Professional Development)
- ✓ Network with other landlords in the area, have your ear to the ground to see what other landlords may know about HMO compliance checks in the area

- ✓ Keep your tenants happy, a disgruntled tenant is all you need to have the council turn up and check everything when you are least expecting it
- ✓ Make regular inspections, check each room against a checklist to cover all the hazards, record it and keep copies 'on the cloud' in case you are asked for them
- ✓ Keep regular fire alarm logs
- ✓ Respond to maintenance issues quickly and communicate everything well to your tenants
- ✓ Always co-operate with the council, if they know you are a co-operative landlord, they will be easier on you
- ✓ Make sure you have all your compliance in place and if you have an agent then it is your job to make sure they do too

Homes Fit for Human Habitation Act 2019

This new law means a tenant can apply to court to bring actions without having to go via the Council if they feel that their property (room) is not fit for human habitation. This new law can also award damages which can relate to the WHOLE LENGTH OF THE TENANCY

Chapter 13 - My Council 'FINE'

So, this is a long story that I will try and summarise and the reason I am telling it is, so you understand that Civil Penalties do really exist, because I had one. The fine was for a whopping £25,000, which made me ill (I was starting a new business and had to put it all on hold) and threw my world into turmoil for three months of my life; it's something I will never forget. And in the end, as I will explain later, I had done nothing wrong. I was not a 'rogue landlord' and I had been treated wrongly, and outside of the Council's own guidelines on Civil Penalties. The whole thing was eventually dropped but that was not before having to go through a stressful and unnecessary situation. Several consultants I had to employ to help me with it all, concluded I had done nothing wrong, but the whole thing had taught me some really hard lessons which I am now going to pass onto you so you don't have to go through what I did.

Lesson 1: Make sure your INSURANCE is totally bullet proof and includes LEGAL COVER, not just a helpline. This will help if this ever happens to you and the Council come calling. Legal representation on HMOs is specialist and therefore EXPENSIVE. My whole legal bill came to just over £2,500 and I had no LEGAL COVER

Lesson 2: Whenever you create an HMO or if you buy one to rent out and it does NOT require a licence (i.e. under 5 occupants etc) then ALWAYS ask the Council to come out and inspect the property before you let it. NEVER work under the radar and if they ask you to change something you think is unreasonable, just DO IT, they will keep you on their radar like nothing on earth and will probably keep tabs on you. I know this happens. They will normally come out and inspect it FOR FREE. When you have done that and you have the green light, get EVERYTHING IN WRITING as rules change and Officers change and sometimes Officers say different things too, sometimes even the same Officer can say something different to another landlord. Scary but true. Just make sure you have your own back covered in case they come after you in the future.

If you have learned nothing else from this book, then please carry out those two steps above in Lessons 1 & 2 and you will thank me forever should you need to fall back on it.

I thought I knew the rules properly, I thought I had followed everything to the letter and I would NEVER do anything to put tenants at risk but I had made a major mistake and followed the WRONG GUIDELINES that I was sent by the Council. I will talk you through what happened as you can see how this could happen to anyone.

In context, I had worked alongside the Council for many years in my role as Residential Services Manager for the University. Indeed, we would inspect HMOs together (I would have to give them access etc) and I learned an awful lot. They would know me by my first name. They would invite me to meetings and seminars and ask me to do talks. I thought they were on 'my side'.

At the time I owned two BTL HMOs in one specific road in Wolverhampton and had a R2R in a street just down the road, remarkably similar layouts, all three were four bed non-licensable properties.

In May 2018 (I recall that as it was the day of the anniversary of my dad's death) I was asked to attend an inspection of my BTLs which I duly did. The Council met me and asked my tenants some questions about the tenancy agreement (joint or separate tenancies); my tenancy was a joint one. They checked the windows and said all was ok. They said I did NOT need a fire door on the kitchen and I only needed smoke alarms hardwired in circulation areas and kitchen which is what I had. On the way out the Council officer said, "but of course if you change to separate lets then you will be required to install smoke alarms in all rooms and a fire door on the kitchen." This I questioned but she assured me the rules were different if the lets were done differently (i.e.

individual tenancies) as the risk would be higher. She said that my HMO would indeed be classed as 'bedsits'.

Coincidentally at the time of the inspection a friend of mine who has a very lead role in the Residential Landlord's Association (RLA) was witness to the inspection and heard everything said.

Armed with this 'new' information that individual lets now constituted 'bedsits' for the purpose of their HMO Regulations (as identified in LACORS) I realised that my R2R HMO would not meet the criteria as I had let the tenants in on individual agreements and they had not known each other before they moved in.

I had to decide to hand back my R2R HMO which I could as I was not tied into a contract and anyway my students' contracts were finishing the following month.

So at the end of May 2018 I met with the owner and I discussed the options with him, I either had to have all fire doors fitted (downstairs mainly) and a full integrated alarm system, or I would have no choice but to hand the property back. The landlord said that he did not want fire doors fitting to the house and he would rather have the property back.

So, on 31st May I hand delivered my notice to his house, to hand the property back on 30th June. My tenants appeared to be moving on anyway although one tenant dragged his heels and I housed him into another HMO.

I began the process of cleaning it and emptying it.

And then on 22nd June 2018 (8 days before keys hand back) the Council carried out a so called 'proactive inspection' of several houses in the area to assess HMOs and identify any that were not meeting regulations. Yes, you guessed it, mine was one of them. As two of the tenants had already vacated, it was not actually an HMO in its legal sense at the time of inspection.

The Council officers spoke to the only tenant in the house at the time; he lived in the room at the front, downstairs. He let them in, and they asked him questions about his tenancy agreement. They also checked on windows downstairs and extraction in the kitchen. They asked if I was a good landlord and attended to repairs quickly to which he said I did (he wrote me a lovely reference later). I knew nothing about any of this, I had not been asked to let anyone into the other rooms upstairs (remember they asked me to the meeting before at my other HMOs). So, they left, they had not inspected all the rooms as all the rooms were locked and two of the tenants had gone anyway. No inspection, nothing.

However, the letter I received on 25th June regarding their 'inspection' concluded I had NO SMOKE DETECTION at all. This was wholly untrue as I had one ground and first floor communal areas as standard and they were hardwired in, just like my other HMOs that had passed with flying colours.

In panic and thinking I must have been mistaken I drove very quickly over to the HMO with the maintenance guy and there they were, two hardwired smoke alarms which we then tested and were ok. What was going on?

The letter I had received also went on to say they had done an HHSRS inspection and that there were Category 1 and 2 hazards which had to be attended to in 28 days. This was going to be difficult as I was handing back keys on 30th June to the landlord and the property had been placed on the market with a Letting Agency for letting to a family. So how could I possibly comply with the instruction to install smoke alarms in ALL rooms and fit fire doors?

Another letter accompanied that one 'inviting' me to an interview under the POLICE AND CRIMINAL EVIDENCE ACT. Now I do not know whether you are familiar with any of these things, but I certainly was not, and I was terrified. I had many calls with many advisers, mostly telling me NOT to go as the Council would try to incriminate me further and if

I did go, I would have to answer 'no comment' until I got further representation.

Days passed as I tried to get some help (remember me saying about make sure you have LEGAL COVER on your insurance policy?). I had 14 days to come up with something fast but all the legal people either wanted several thousand pounds, did not call me back or said it was not something they could deal with, it was so complex.

So, I told the Council I would be not accepting their 'invite' to the PACE interview, I had no choice. Seemingly, that made things worse because several months later they decided to issue me with this massive penalty and say that I had been 'obstructive' in their investigations by not attending their PACE interview.

Luckily for me I had good friends on my side and through the power of networking had found the guy that wrote LACORS. He went through all the 'allegations' made against me and concluded I had done nothing wrong because I had been given a set of 'guidance' to follow which wasn't in fact a set of legal rules. The interpretation had been particularly difficult, and I had put fire prevention measures in place. But I was not out of the woods yet.

So, in comes Barrister Julian Hunt whom I had the pleasure of meeting sometime after I had the Civil Penalty of £25,000 drop on my doorstep. Incidentally, this was done by hand, at 4.15pm on a Friday afternoon, giving me NO chance to get any advice about it until Monday. It was a particularly stressful weekend I can tell you. I collapsed in a heap and my then 14-year-old Lily scraped me up and told me everything would be ok. I believed her, I knew I had not done what I had been accused of doing, or not doing.

Julian visited me in Wolverhampton and was disgusted about how the Council had treated me, given my background and how we had worked together in the past on the general improvements of housing in the area. He also couldn't believe the amount of the fine as it was totally disproportionate to their alleged 'offences'. In addition to that the Council had told me that they were going to use a ZERO TOLERANCE policy against me (many Councils do this now) which really means an 'on the spot fine'. However, I later found out that at the time my fine was issued, this 'policy' had not even been ratified by the Council's cabinet. So therefore, they had acted outside of their powers.

The nature of the 'fines' now are that they can be 'on the spot' and up to £30k for each 'offence'. Which is quite scary. The documents they send you, tell you that if you do not or cannot pay them, they can levy a 'charge' against any assets, i.e. your property. Given that this property wasn't even mine, it could have meant that it would have been put against my own personal house or that I could have been forced to sell it.

Bizarrely too in the letter from the Council saying why the fine was £25,000, they said that it was not only because I had been 'obstructive' but because I was a landlord who 'should have known better' as I had been a long-standing landlord in the area.

My representations were made to the Council by Julian Hunt. A long wait for another 28 days followed for their decision which finally came, and they dropped the whole case saying they had made a 'mistake'. They said their mistake was in giving me 28 days to rectify the fire safety measures when this was incorrect, and it should have been an immediate fine. In other words, they did not really know what they were doing and handled it badly. My whole world was put on hold by a graduate Environmental Health Officer who decided I had broken the law and in fact I had not.

So they didn't put me on a 'rogue landlord' list but had this not been dropped then that could have been their action and I would have had further costs to take this further to appeal in a Tribunal hearing which I would have done without hesitation. I am not able to recover any of my costs in this situation as it was all done in-house via Civil Penalty. Remember too that the Councils have been given the powers to issue these penalties how they see fit AND KEEP THE MONEY IN THEIR OWN DEPARTMENTS. Which means more enforcers of course.

Another way of keeping on the right side of the Council is to join any Accreditation Schemes they have in their area. This is how they keep you 'on the radar' but if they do come knocking, they may be more lenient on you. The one in my area is called Rent with Confidence and awards you a set of stars in accordance with their criteria. Good to know and should be displayed on your noticeboard when you show prospective tenants' round.

To conclude, if your strategy is either BTL or R2R HMO you must be very clear that if there is a Council inspection of your property (which can follow if any of your tenants complain of anything), then YOU will receive a large fine if you don't know how to do things correctly. Furthermore, this can happen to you even if the house is not YOURS.

This is YOUR HMO journey. Learn it properly, listen to the experts and your business will be successful

<Blank Page>

Chapter 14 - Stories And Bloopers

Sometimes in property things happen that you cannot quite believe, we are, after all, dealing with human beings. Over a period of well over 20 years there have been quite a few of these, some are quite sad, some will make you cross, and some are just funny.

At the time of writing this the whole world is going through a global Pandemic and this is presenting many difficulties for landlords and tenants alike. Nothing could have prepared us for the onslaught of this awful situation, I will mention it again later.

Story: The day my tenants walked to my house

Important to note because I learned a very valuable lesson, which was MAKE SURE YOUR ADDRESS ON THE APPLICATION FORM IS CORRECT. At the time I had a Lettings Shop in Wolverhampton and somehow sent an old application form out to four tenants who were going to be moving into a managed property in the summer. When they did not arrive on time for their appointment to sign contracts etc we called them and were reassured they were 'on their way'. A good half an hour later we checked again and still no sign.... Because they were on the way to MY house. I had left the address on from when I used to work from home (though I never met tenants there as that wouldn't have been allowed in a small cul-de-sac), how we both laughed when we realised they were nearly at MY FRONT DOOR. Happily, they saw the funny side too.

I managed to do it again one day when I was asked for the postcode (of the property) on 'Spare Room'. I put my own house postcode by mistake, just a typo but she, as well, began making the journey to my house. Funnily enough my house number and the house number to the HMO were the same so when I said "are you at No 19?" she said "yes." but of course was at the wrong one and we wondered why we couldn't see each other.

Story: Why am I getting my tenant's post?

A nice guy from Turkey moved into one of my rooms, pretty much straight off a plane. He paid me and all was ok, I organised a desk etc and did the Health and Safety talk about smoking/fire alarms etc and pointed out the Manager's Details sellotaped to the back of the front door (which is a legal requirement). He acknowledged all of that and thanked me. Then, a week later I started getting his post AT MY HOUSE. I asked him about it, and he explained "oh I thought the notice on the back of the door was the address where I live".

Story: The headless birds

In our line of work, we do have to understand cultural differences and I thought I had most of them covered. Until this one. The tenants, who were from Cyprus, had all gone home at the end of their tenancy, the property left in a reasonable condition. Until I opened the freezer. There in the bottom were TWO fully feathered, very stiff, PHEASANTS glued to the compartment with ice. Apparently, these Cypriots believed very firmly on living from the land and used to go out shooting them. I had to come up with a way of getting the poor things out and the only way I could do that was to defrost the freezer. There was no way I could ask a cleaner to do something I didn't want to do myself so I had to roll up my sleeves, literally and pull them out feet first, parts of the birds staying stuck, parts coming away, you can probably imagine so I won't go into any more details. Job done and said pheasants disposed of in their own 'body bags' and out they went in the refuse. Thankfully, it was bin day the following day.

Story: Our Housemate is not Responding

This is a sad story and some of it does prove how importance due diligence is. Sometimes I am just too soft and gave this guy the benefit of the doubt. So, here is the story. A guy who was Eastern European (I have forgotten the actual country) applied for a room and told me he had a job at a nearby Car factory. It was a Friday afternoon and he seemed desperate to move in. Application completed, deposit given, previous landlord check done, he told me his reference from his employer would follow the next week. So, he moved in and then the complaints started from the fellow housemates about his drinking habits, morning noon and night. No reference appeared and it became clear he had no job; he would just stay home all-day drinking. He had seemed a very reasonable guy, but I soon realised that I had been duped. Efforts to collect his rent resulted in him hiding from me literally, behind a neighbour's hedge. I finally got to see him about a week later and talked to him very sternly about his lack of rent and the complaints I had received. He admitted he had no job. As I spoke to him, he began leaning against the doorframe and sweating profusely, something did not seem right so I stopped in my tracks and suggested he sought medical advice which he said he would. I agreed to check on him in a week.

Sometime later the following week I had a few missed calls from a fellow housemate which I could not answer immediately. I called her back and she said she was terribly upset as the guy I had described was in the kitchen and was 'not responding'. I asked her to call an ambulance and I got over there immediately. It seems the poor guy had been making himself a drink and had literally died, standing up. When the paramedics arrived, he was already 'going cold' and rigor mortis had already started to set in. It was like he had just 'switched off'. The other housemates and I were all in a bit of shock, it took some time to sink in. I called his previous landlord and they gave me his next of kin details which for some reason I did not have. I had to make 'that call' to tell them their family member had died. This guy was 57 and had family in his home country.

What followed then was a few calls with his Embassy to repatriate him back home and a company who called me saying that his belongings would be collected. I met two men there who had a van and they took all his things away including laptops and phones. They had no ID at all, and I was told just to hand it all over which I did. A very strange experience. I left the room empty for several months after that out of respect and handed the property back to the landlord (it was due to go back anyway it was a R2R).

There are countless other oddities that went on from finding naked tenants in the house (despite being told we were going in), a tenant being locked INSIDE a bathroom when the lock broke, tenants complaining of other housemates' 'noisy sex' and a strange situation at the university when I was called into interview a student who had attacked a fellow student and was still holding the bottle she did it with.

Chapter 15 - The Future

2020 PANDEMIC

This is not a chapter I intended to write when I started out, however events have started to emerge very rapidly in the last few weeks, so I felt it right to record it for 'historic' purposes.

This is by far the most serious, life-changing event the world has seen since the Spanish flu of 1918. As I write the UK is in lockdown and we are only allowed to go out of our homes to exercise once a day and to buy essential food. The impact on the world economy is huge, let alone the death rate globally. All businesses are closed except those which are keeping the country going. Massive companies like Jaguar Land Rover and other manufacturers are closed including huge retailers like Argos, Primark, the list is endless. All bars, cafes and restaurants are closed. The world is heading for a massive global crisis like never seen before. We are not at the top of the 'peak' of the outbreak yet, worse is still to come. The strain on the NHS is almost unbearable. All schools and educational institutions have been closed for a few weeks now. Massive emergency hospitals are being set up in record breaking time in London (The Nightingale),

Manchester, Birmingham in large complexes like music venues.

People working from home are trying to get by on Government handouts and Boris Johnson has pledged that the Government will reimburse employers 80% of their employees' wages and is in a scheme called 'furlough'. Many people like the self-employed have had to turn to state benefits to keep food on the table. The Serviced Accommodation sector is on its knees, some providers are offering their places free or low cost to NHS or 'key' workers (like social care, shop workers, delivery drivers, food chain etc). Our Prime Minister too has now been taken ill and is in intensive care in London.

The world has become very uncertain however I think in all of this that the HMO 'industry' will survive as there will be an ongoing need for low-cost accommodation that we can offer. There are even talks about the divorce rate and relationship breakdowns going up because of people being cooped up together for days on end. Tenant 'profiles' are likely to change and we will see a whole new wave of people relying on benefits to pay their rents and we should embrace that and help where we can and refrain from using the 'sorry NO DSS' phrase in our adverts.

The housing market will of course be affected too, and many might have to sell properties that they might have kept otherwise, to clear debt they have built up during lockdown. Lenders are not currently lending, and surveyors are not currently surveying so everything is on hold. But in an uncertain world, property is likely to be hit, and prices will come falling.

Which will bring new opportunities.

I hope my next book about Management will bring us all better news.

<Blank Page>

Chapter 16 - The HMO Training Academy

The ACADEMY was created in 2019 by myself and my business partner Georgina Smallwood. Together we have over 20 years of real-life management experience. Georgina has run her own R2R properties and now manages HMOs for other people in her Agency, Flying the Nest Properties.

The Academy mentors' new investors who have an interest in growing a portfolio of HMO Properties and we can tailor the services to you.

What our services can do for you:

So far, I have saved investors thousands of pounds by steering them away from wrong decisions and costly mistakes. Here are a few examples:

CASE STUDY 1: David lives in Luton and was looking for R2R opportunities. He had a baby on the way and wanted to quit his day job in a factory. He had been looking for R2R deals endlessly and through networking found someone to help him who lives in an investment area he was interested in which is Suffolk. David's journey to his investment area took him an hour and 40 minutes but he wanted to do the viewings himself. We came up with a plan so he could do 'accompanied' viewings whilst his friend did a show round on video in real time. It saves David a day of wasted time on a motorway and more time to look for new deals

CASE STUDY 2: Chris found a R2R deal in Southampton and had undergone 'some' training with a mentor. He was struggling to rent the rooms out, so I gave him lots of tips to make the rooms look better. On chatting I asked him if he was on the licence (7 beds) but he said no as the landlord is the licence holder. Christopher was breaking the law by not being added to the licence as the 'manager'. He soon sorted this out and avoided a massive fine of up to £30,000 and a listing on the rogue landlord register and being banned from managing properties.

CASE STUDY 3: Sue contacted me to say she had decided to reduce her rents on her property, so she did not have to pay the bills anymore because the tenants were using too much electric and gas. We talked about ways to reduce her heating costs by using an App on her phone and a controller like Nest or to put an over-use clause in their contracts. By removing gas and electricity from their contracts this could cause problems in the property such as mould and arguments. She was also thinking of selling and I advised her that if she reduced the rent, she may well receive a lower valuation. She thanked me very much and realised I had saved her a load of money.

CASE STUDY 4: Rob called me to say he had identified an HMO he wanted to buy in Balsall Heath in Birmingham. The house did not need a lot of work doing on it and already had fire doors but had not been used as an HMO. He was excited and was prepared to pay the £280k for it. This was for four, possibly five bedrooms. He wanted to buy it because he knew the people selling and he lived not far from there. I pointed out that there were better deals to be had and indeed in some areas you can buy four bedroomed houses for half that price and achieve similar rents. I advised him to work out his Return on Investment (ROI) on that kind of capital expenditure and to look in other areas. He also has Article 4 looming so if he did not complete on time then he would not be able to run it as an HMO anyway.

So you can see from these examples that just by talking something through and having someone to 'watch your back' can indeed save you money and that is what you will be able to achieve via mentorship.

Mentorship will include:

- ✓ Ongoing support on a one to one basis and modules in an on-line training portal
- ✓ Access to our WhatsApp and Facebook groups for loads of tips and advice

- ✓ Action planning and accountability to help you to reach your goals
- ✓ Live Deal Sourcing
- ✓ Access to our intensive training courses

www.hmotrainingacademy.co.uk

info@hmotrainingacademy.co.uk

TESTIMONIALS

These are genuine comments from people I have mentored.

"Great mentorship call today with Marie Ellis. She gave me plenty of HMO advice and tips. Maris has given me great confidence in finding my first R2R deal!!"

GAB SANDHU, LONDON

"As buy to let investors we were looking for some guidance and found Marie whilst stalking online Facebook groups. She had a plethora of ideas for designs and layouts within our project. She is just on the end of the phone and having her in our team has given us the confidence to tackle this new project. We can't wait to show her the results."

MOSES AND CLAIRE ELLIOTT, WIRRAL

"Had a call with Marie Ellis earlier today. She is so knowledgeable, helpful, easy to talk to and was able to answer all the questions I had been struggling to find answers for. Thanks again Marie!"

KAFILAH LAWAL

"Marie gave me lots of advice with my R2R HMO. Her knowledge and expertise in this area is amazing, couldn't have done it without her."

CHRISTIAN LIDDLE, SOUTHAMPTON

"Marie Ellis is a lovely person and has a great vibrant personality. I would highly recommend this company if anyone of you are looking for some professional help and this company and her team are one of the best if the not the best in the area."

MARIA GUTEHALL, SWEDEN

"Thank you so much for helping me with a current HMO issue and highlighting some areas that could help the situation and future ones if overlooked. Get booking people, Marie is so easy to talk to and has a wealth of knowledge, lovely to be given some help with nothing expected in return, thanks again Marie, very kind of you."

ARTI PANCHOLI, BIRMINGHAM

"Just had an hour one to one with Marie, really insightful and incredibly useful information that you wouldn't find on a free property course event! I would highly recommend her to help you get your property business going."

JUNAL BARBOZA, NOTTINGHAM

"Marie is a brilliant mentor. She is full of very useful information to get you on track if you are starting out in r2r/HMOs. She has a great personality and will give you facts rather than waffle. I would highly recommend Marie for anyone starting out in their journey and needs someone to work alongside them to reach their goals."

SAMANTHA MAY, BIRMINGHAM

To my beautiful Toby who died just after my book was completed, aged 14. I spent many hours writing it with him by my side. May he be chasing postmen, burying bones, and chasing flies forever in the sky, until we meet again. I couldn't have wished for a better dog. Xxx

And finally, here is the lovely and talented MEMORY (MEMZ) MEDZIMA whom I had the privilege to mentor in Telford recently. I had planned an hour with her, and we talked for three! She unfortunately lost her life due to pneumonia on 15th March 2020. God bless you Memz.

Printed in Great Britain
by Amazon

26479208R00075